ACCOUNTING
MADE EASY
financial
accounting

Kevin A.

Table of contents

INTRODUCTION

What is accounting?

Accounting is the systematic and comprehensive recording of financial transactions pertaining to a business. Accounting can also be referred to as the art of recording, summarizing, reporting, and analyzing financial transactions.

There are various branches of accounting. They include;

- Financial accounting. It involves the maintenance of financial information used by both internal and external end users.

- Cost accounting. This branch of accounting deals with cost ascertainment and determination of selling price of commodities.

- Tax accounting. This branch of accounting deals with the determination of taxable income and tax liability.

- Management accounting. Is a branch of accounting that applies cost accounting principles and provides information for managerial decision making.

Users of Accounting information

- ◆ Managers – They need information about the financial state of the business' current and future, so as to manage business efficiently and to make effective control and planning decisions.

- ◆ Suppliers – They would wish to know the liquidity position of the firm, that is, its ability to meet its obligations as and when they fall due.

- ◆ Government – It would want to know the business' profits in order to determine tax payable and taxable income.

- ◆ Customers – They are interested in the going concern of the business i.e the ability of the business to be in operation in the foreseeable future and provide them with goods and services.

- ◆ Shareholders/owners – They would wish to know how efficiently their business is being managed so as to determine the level of dividends they are likely to receive.

- ◆ Employees – They are interested in financial information of the business for the following purposes;

  a) To assess job security.

  b) To determine the level of benefits they are likely to receive.

c) To negotiate for higher wages.

◆ Lenders – They are interested in the solvency of the firm, ability to keep up with interest payments and eventually repay the principal.

Accounting concepts and principles

- **Prudence** – Prudence requires that accountants should exercise a degree of caution in the adopting of policies and significant estimates such that the assets and income of the entity are not overstated whereas liabilities and expenses are not understated.

- **Matching concept** – it requires that expenses incurred by an organization must be charged to the income statement in the accounting period in which the revenue to which those expenses relate, is earned.

- **Business entity** – It emphasizes that any personal expenses incurred by owners of a business will not appear in the income statement of the entity; hence transactions and balances of a business entity are to be accounted for separately from its owners.

- **Accrual concept** – It requires that incomes and expenses must be recorded in the accounting period to which they relate, rather than on cash basis. An exception to this rule is the cash flow statement whose main purpose is to present the cash flow effects of transactions during an accounting period.

- **Duality** – It is a fundamental convention of accounting that necessitates the recognition of all aspects of accounting transactions. It is the underlying basis for double entry accounting system, i.e Debit (dr) and Credit (cr).

- **Going concern** – Financial statements are prepared assuming that a business entity will continue to operate in the foreseeable future without the need or intention on the part of management to liquidate the entity or cease its operational activities.

Terms used in accounting

- ✓ **Assets** – Resources owned by the business to which money value can be calculated. For example, vehicles, land, debtors, cash in hand, cash at bank, prepaid expenses, accrued income. There are two types of assets; **Non current assets**, which are assets affected to save the business for a long period of time, usually more than a year. And **current assets** which are assets affected to save the business for a short period of time, usually less than a year.

- ✓ **Liabilities** – The business' existing debts and obligations owed. There are of two types; **long term liabilities** which are not due for at least one year e.g long term loans, debentures, mortgages et cetera, and **current liabilities** which are due in one year or less e.g bank overdraft, creditors, trade payables.

- ✓ **Debtors** – Those who owe money to the business. They are individuals/entities that acquire goods on credit from the business.
- ✓ **Creditors** – Those who supply goods and services on credit to the business.
- ✓ **Capital** – The amount on the owner's interest in the firm after deducting liabilities from assets. (Resources to start a business).
- ✓ **Purchases** – Acquisition of stock or goods for resale.
- ✓ **Expenses** – Cost incurred to generate income e.g rent, wages, carriage inwards, carriage outwards.
- ✓ **Return inwards** – Goods returned by customers if they do not meet the required specification. They are deducted from sales.
- ✓ **Return outwards** – They are goods returned to suppliers. They are deducted from purchases.
- ✓ **Income** – Revenue generated by a business from trading activities e.g sales income, discount received, gain on asset disposal.

Accounting Equation

It's a mathematical expression showing the relationship between assets, liabilities and capital. When starting a business, capital is used to acquire assets. Sometimes the capital is not enough to finance the assets and therefore the business acquire liability. A business can combine capital and liabilities to get assets.

Illustration: Assets = Capital + Liabilities

$$A = C + L \qquad\qquad C = A - L$$
$$C = A - C$$

Unit 1

Recording of Transactions and Double Entry Concept

What is double entry?

Double entry – Every business transaction has a 2 fold effect on the business i.e it affects the best in two ways.

This forms the basis of double entry concept which states that "for every debit entry there is a corresponding credit entry."

Illustration:

Debit(Dr)	Credit(Cr)

The ledger a/c

A ledger account is divided into:

I. The left hand side (debit side). It records increase in assets, increase in expenses, increase in drawings, increase in return inwards and decrease in income and liabilities.
II. The right hand side (Credit side). It records increase in liabilities, increase in income, increase in return outwards and decrease in assets and expenses.

Each side of the ledger is divided into:

a) Date column. Which records the date when the transaction occurred.
b) Particulars. Which records the details of the transaction or corresponding account to be debit or credit.
c) Folio. Which records the page number of the transaction in the source document or book of original entry where transaction is obtained.
d) Amount. Which records the amount involved in the transaction.

Note

Assets are debits with increases and credits with decreases.

Liabilities are debits with decreases and credits with increases.

Sales are credits.

Purchases are debits.

Capital is debit with decreases and credit with increases.

Drawings are debits.

Expenses are debits with increases and credits with decreases.

Return inwards are debits and return outwards are credits.

Incomes are debits with decreases and credits with increases.

Effects of transactions

Date	Transaction	Effects	A/c Dr	A/c Cr
1 Jan	Started business with $ 100, 000. Increases cash at bank.	Increase in capital. Increase in bank.	Bank	Capital
2 Jan	Withdrew cash worth $ 100, 000 for office use.	Increase in cash. Decrease in bank.	Cash	Bank
4 Jan	Paid wages in cash $ 10, 000.	Increase in wages. Decrease in cash.	Wages	Cash
6 Jan	Bought goods worth $ 200, 000 on credit from Alice.	Increase in purchases. Creditor increase.	Purchases	Alice
8 Jan	Returned goods worth $10, 000 for Alice.	Return outwards increase. Creditors decrease.	Alice	Return outwards
10 Jan	Bought goods worth $	Increase in purchase	Purchases	Bank

	250,000 paying by check.	s. Decrease in bank.		
11 Jan	Sold goods worth $ 400,000 on credit to Jefferson.	Increase in sales. Increase in debtors.	Jefferson	Sales
12 Jan	Jefferson returned goods worth $ 10,000.	Increase in return inwards. Decrease in debtors.	Return inwards	Jefferson
15 Jan	Paid Alice $ 190,000 by check.	Decrease in creditors. Decrease in bank.	Alice	Bank
17 Jan	Received commissi on income $ 50,000 by check.	Income increase. Bank increase.	Bank	Commissi on income

Example 1

The following shows Stephen's list of transactions in the month of January;

1 Jan – Started a business with $ 800,000 cash at hand

2 Jan – Paid rent for premises $ 20,000 cash

3 Jan – Banked $ 600,000

4 Jan – Bought office furniture worth $ 80,000 cash

5 Jan – Bought goods worth $ 300,000 on credit from John

6 Jan – Took goods worth $ 10,000 for personal use

7 Jan – Returned goods worth $ 5,000 to John

8 Jan – Sold goods worth $ 200,000 by check

9 Jan – Paid John the total amount due on his account by check

10 Jan – Bought goods worth $ 500,000 paying by check

11 Jan – Sold goods worth $ 600,000 on credit to William

12 Jan – Received a check of $ 200,000 from William

13 Jan – Paid wages in cash $ 15,000

15 Jan – William paid a total amount due on his account in cash.

Required: show effects of transactions.

Solution

Date	Transaction	Effects	A/c Dr	A/c Cr
1 Jan		Increase in capital. Increase in cash.	Cash	Capital
2 Jan		Increase in expense. Decrease in cash.	Expense	Cash
3 Jan		Increase in bank. Decrease in cash.	Bank	Cash
4 Jan		Furniture increase. Decrease in cash.	Furniture	Cash
5 Jan		Increase in purchases Increase in creditors	Purchases	Creditors (John)
6 Jan		Increase in drawings. Purchases decrease.	Drawings	Purchases
7 Jan		Return outwards increase. Creditors decrease.	Creditors (John)	Return outwards
8 Jan		Increase in bank.	Bank	Sales

		Increase in sales.		
9 Jan		Creditors decrease. Decrease in bank.	Creditors (John)	Bank
10 Jan		Increase in purchases Decrease in bank.	Purchases	Bank
11 Jan		Increase in sales. Increase in debtors.	William (debtors)	Sales
12 Jan		Increase in bank. Debtors decrease.	Bank	William (debtors)
13 Jan		Increase in wages. Decrease in cash.	Wages	Cash
15 Jan		Increase in cash. Debtors decrease.	Cash	William (debtors)

Example 2

Write the various ledger accounts needed in the books of K. Omarion to record the following:

1st May. Opened a business with $ 20, 000 in the bank.

2nd May. Bought premises for $ 8, 000.

5th May. Bought motor van worth $ 2, 000 on credit from J. Hernandez.

7th May. Bought goods from R. Miller for resale at $ 800.

12th May. Bought goods for $ 500.

13th May. Sold goods for $ 600.

15th May. Sold goods on credit to M. Roberts worth $ 700.

16th May. Received a loan from bank $ 12, 000.

17th May. Paid by check to J. Hernandez.

20th May. Paid wages and salaries $ 1000 by check.

21st May. Received a check from M. Roberts $ 700.

30th May. Paid sundry expenses by check $ 100.

Solution:

Dr.		Bank a/c				Cr
		$				$
1st May	Capital	20,000	17th May	J. Hernandez		2,000
16th May	Bank loan	12,000	20th May	Wages and salaries		1,000
21st May	M. Roberts	700	30th May	Sundry expenses.		100
			31st May	Balance c/f		29,600
		32,700				**32,700**
1 Apr	Balance b/f	29,600				

Dr.		Capital a/c				Cr.
		$				$
			1st May	Bank.		20,000
31 May	Balance c/f.	20,000				
		20,000				**20,000**
			1st April	Balance b/f		20,000

Dr.		Cash a/c				Cr.
		$				$
13th May	Sales	600	2nd May	Premises		8,000
			7th May	Purchases		800
31st May	Balance c/f	8,700	12th May	Purchases		500
		9,300				**9,300**
			1st April	Balance b/f.		8,700

Dr.		Premises a/c				Cr.	
		$				$	
5th May	Cash	8, 000		31st May	Balance c/f	8, 000	
		8, 000				**8, 000**	
1st April	Balance b/f	8, 000					

Dr.		Motor van a/c				Cr.	
		$				$	
5th May	J. Hernandez	2, 000		31st May	Balance c/f	2, 000	
		2, 000				**2, 000**	
1st April	Balance b/f	2, 000					

Dr.		J. Hernandez a/c				Cr.	
		$				$	
17th May	Bank	2, 000		5th May	Motor van	2, 000	
		2, 000				**2, 000**	

Dr.		Purchases a/c				Cr.	
		$				$	
7th May	Cash	800					
12th May	Cash	500		31st May	Balance c/f	1, 300	
		1, 300				**1, 300**	
1st April	Balance b/f	1, 300					

Dr.		Sales a/c				Cr.
		$				$
			13th May	Cash		600
31st May	Balance c/f	1, 300	15th May	M. Roberts		700
		1, 300				1, 300
			1st April	Balance b/f		1, 300

Dr.		M. Roberts a/c				Cr.
		$				$
31st May	Sales	700	21st May	Bank		700
		700				700

Dr.		Bank loan a/c				Cr.
		$				$
31st May	Balance c/f	12, 000	16th May	Bank		12, 000
		12, 000				12, 000
			1st April	Balance b/f		12, 000

Dr.		Wages & salaries a/c				Cr.
		$				$
20th May	Bank	1, 000	31st May	Balance c/f		1, 000
		1, 000				1, 000

Dr.		Sundry expense a/c				Cr.
		$				$
30th May	Bank	100	31st May	Balance c/f		100
		100				100

N/B:

- At the end of the period it is necessary to determine the position of an account. This is done by balancing off an account. To balance an account, the total on the debit and credit sides are determined then the difference between the two sides is determined. This difference is recorded on the side of the account which is lesser and it is recorded as **balance c/d** or **balance c/f**.
- At the beginning of the next period this will be recorded on the opposite side and it's known as **balance b/d** or **balance b/f**.
- The balances are given names depending on the side of the account which is greater. If the debit side is greater than the credit side, the balance is known as a debit balance and if the credit side is greater than the debit side, the balance is known as a credit balance.
- A debit balance is **c/d** on the credit side and **b/d** on the debit side while a credit balance is **c/d** on the debit side and **b/d** on the credit side.

A single line is put above the totals and double lines below the totals.

The Trial Balance

- It is a financial statement used to check the arithmetic accuracy of a ledger account.
- It has two main columns, the debit column and the credit column.
- All the debit balances are recorded on the debit column and all credit balances are recorded on the credit column.
- If proper double entry has been done the total on the debit and credit sides must be equal, i.e The Trial Balance **MUST** balance.

Uses of The Trial Balance

I. To check for errors in recording of transactions.
II. It provides information for preparing final books of a/c, i.e The Income statement and The Balance sheet (Statement of financial position).
III. It summarizes all the business transactions.

Format:

R. Miller
Trial Balance
As at 31st January

Particulars	Dr.	Cr.
Capital		xxxx
Bank	xxxxx	
Cash	xxx	
Motor vehicle	xxx	
Purchases	xxxx	
Rent	xxxx	
Debtor	xxx	
Sales		xxxx
Wages	xx	
Return outwards		xxx
Drawings	xxxx	
Commission income		xx
Return inwards	xx	
	XXXXXX	**XXXXXX**

Example

The following are the first 12 transactions of a new business:

Feb. 01 Put $ 40, 000 into a business bank account.

Feb. 01 Paid rent $ 1, 400 by check.

Feb. 02 Paid $ 19, 000 for fixed assets paying by check.

Feb. 03 Bought goods for resale $ 5, 500 paying by check.

Feb. 06 Bought stationery for $ 650 paying by check.

Feb. 07 Sold goods for $ 3, 400 and immediately banked the check.

Feb. 09 Paid wages $ 1, 400 paying by check.

Feb. 10 Bought goods for resale $ 6, 000 paying by check.

Feb. 14 Paid insurance premium $ 1, 800 paying by check.

Feb. 15 Sold goods for $ 5, 600 and immediately banked the check.

Feb. 15 Paid wages $ 1, 400 paying by check.

Feb. 15 Sold goods for $ 5, 300 and immediately banked the check.

Required:

i.   Record all transactions in their appropriate ledgers.
ii. Prepare Trial Balance as at 31st February.

Solution

i.

Dr.		Capital a/c				Cr.
		$				$
Balance c/f	40,000		1 Feb.	Bank	40,000
		40,000				**40,000**

Dr.		Rent a/c			Cr.
		$			$
2 Feb.	Bank.	1,400	Balance c/f	1,400
		1,400		**1,400**

Dr.		Purchases a/c			Cr.
		$			$
3 Feb.	Bank	5,500		
10 Feb.	Bank	6,000	Balance c/f	11,500
		11,500		**11,500**

Dr.		Fixed assets a/c			Cr.
		$			$
2 Feb.	Bank	19,000	Balance c/f	19,000
		19,000		**19,000**

Dr.		Insurance premium a/c			Cr.
		$			$
14 Feb.	Bank	1,800	Balance c/f	1,800
		1,800		**1,800**

Dr.		Stationery a/c			Cr.
		$			$
6 Feb.	Bank	650	Balance c/f		650
		650			**650**

Dr.		Wages a/c			Cr.
		$			$
9 Feb.	Bank	1, 400			
15 Feb.	Bank	1, 400	Balance c/f		2, 800
		2, 800			**2, 800**

Dr.		Sales a/c			Cr.
		$			$
			7 Feb.	Bank	3, 400
			15 Feb.	Bank	5, 600
	Balance c/f	14, 300	15 Feb.	Bank	5, 300
		14, 300			**14, 300**

Dr.		Bank a/c			Cr.
		$			$
1 Feb.	Capital	40, 000	1 Feb.	Rent	1, 400
7 Feb.	Sales	3, 400	2 Feb.	Fixed assets	19, 000
15 Feb.	Sales	5, 600	3 Feb.	Purchases	5, 500
15 Feb.	Sales	5, 300	6 Feb.	Stationery	650
			9 Feb.	Wages	1, 400
			10 Feb.	Purchases	6, 000
			14 Feb.	Insurance premium	1, 800
			15 Feb.	Wages	1, 400
				Balance c/f	17, 150
		54, 300			**54, 300**

ii.

18

Trial Balance

As at 31st February

Particulars	Dr. $	Cr. $
Capital		40,000
Bank	17,150	
Purchases	11,500	
Sales		14,300
Wages	2,800	
Stationery	650	
Insurance premium	1,800	
Rent	1,400	
Fixed assets	19,000	
	54,300	**54,300**

Note: When recording transactions in ledger accounts debit the receiver account and credit the giver account. For example, a transaction involving bank and rent accounts. If the bank is the one receiving money you'll debit the bank account while you credit the rent account, i.e in the bank a/c **rent** will be recorded on the debit column and in the rent a/c **bank** will be recorded on the credit column.

Petty Cash book

It's a book of original entry that records petty transactions, i.e cash transactions involving small amounts of money. It mostly record transactions relating to transport, postage, cleaning, miscellaneous expenses, etc.

The reason for maintaining petty cash book is to reduce entry of the main cash book.

At the beginning, petty cashiers receives an amount of money known as petty **cash float**. They use this money to pay for petty expenses and once is finished they receive additional money known as **reimbursement**. This is known as **The Imprest System**.

Format

Petty Cash book

Dr.   Cr.

Receipt	Date	Details	Folio	Voucher no.	Totals	Postage	Miscellaneous	Stationery

Example

The following petty cash book transactions took place in may 2013:

1 May.   Opening balance of $ 200

2 May.   Paid for stationery $ 20

3 May.   Paid taxi fare $ 21

7 May.   Paid for office tea $ 6

13 May.   Paid taxi fare $ 16

15 May.   Paid for stationery $ 15

23 May.   Paid taxi fare $ 16

24 May.   Paid taxi fare $ 17

25 May.   Paid for stationery $ 16

26 May.   Paid for office tea $ 6

26 May.   Paid taxi fare $ 20

27 May.   Paid for stationery $ 10

29 May.   Paid taxi fare $ 18

31 May. Received from the main cashier the amount required to make up the imprest to $ 200

Required: Record the transactions in the petty cash book and use the following 3 headings; stationery, taxi fare and office tea.

Solution

Petty cash book

For the period ended 31/05/2013

Dr.   Cr.

Receipts	Date	Details	Voucher no.	Totals	Stationery	Taxi fare	Office tea
200	1/05/13	Balance b/d					
	2/05/13	Stationery		20	20		
	3/05/13	Taxi fare		21		21	
	7/05/13	Office tea		6			6
	13/05/13	Taxi fare		16		16	
	15/05/13	Stationery		15	15		
	23/05/13	Taxi fare		16		16	
	24/05/13	Taxi fare		17		17	
	25/05/13	Stationery		16	16		
	26/05/13	Office tea		6			6
	26/05/13	Taxi fare		20		20	
	27/05/13	Stationery		10	10		
	29/05/13	Taxi fare		18		18	
181	31/05/13			181			
		Balance c/f		200.	61	108	12
381.				381.			
200	1/06/13	Balance b/f					

CASH BOOK

It's a book of original entry that records cash and bank transactions; the debit side records receipts of cash and checks (movement of cash into the business) and the credit side records payments in cash or check (movement of cash out of the business).

It can also be used as a ledger to complete double entry. A cash book is both a ledger and a book of original entry.

There are several types of cash book. The commonly used types cash book are two, namely; *Two column cash book and Three column cash book.*

Two column cash book

It has two columns for writing amounts on both debit and credit side. These columns are headed as cash and bank.

Contra entry - It is an entry that appear on both sides of the same account or cash book.

Example

The following transactions need to be written in a two column cash book:

1/05/12. Debit balance b/f; Bank $ 5, 000 and cash $ 1 000.

3/05/12. Paid rent by check $ 1, 000.

5/05/12. Received checks from Brian $ 380, William $ 475

6/05/12. Cash sales $ 3, 000.

8/05/12. Paid wages $ 1, 000 by cash.

10/05/12. Paid the following suppliers;   Frank $ 600 and Joan $ 550.

12/05/12. Bought equipment worth $ 14, 000 paying by check.

20/05/12. Cash sales $ 4, 000.

24/05/12. Paid $ 3, 000 of the cash into the bank.

29/05/12. Paid wages of $ 1, 100 by cash.

30/06/12. Paid rent $ 1, 000 by check.

Solution:

Two column cash book

for the year ended 30/05/12

Dr.   Cr.

Date	Details	Folio	Cash $	Bank $	Date	Details	Folio	Cash $	Bank $
1/05/12	Balance b/f		1,000	5,000	3/05/12	Rent			1,000
5/05/12	Brian			380	8/05/12	Wages		1,000	
5/05/12	William			475	10/05/12	Frank		600	
6/05/12	Sales		3,000						
20/05/12	Sales		4,000		10/05/12	Joan		550	
					12/05/12	Equipment			14,000
24/05/12	Cash	C		3,000	24/05/12	Bank	C	3,000	
					29/05/12	Wages		1,100	
					30/05/12	Rent			1,000
	Balance c/f			7,145.		Balance c/f		1,750.	
			8,000	16,000				8,000	16,000

Three column cash book

It has three main columns i.e the cash column, bank column and discount column.

Discount allowed is an expense and appears on the debit side of the cash book while discount received is an income and appears on the credit side.

The recognition of discounts in the cash book is not part of the double entry and therefore the double entry for discounts should be;

Debit discount allowed a/c and credit Debtors cash a/c

Debit creditors cash a/c and credit Discount received a/c

Format

Three column cash book

Date	Details	Folio	D. Allowed	Cash	Bank	Date	Details	Folio	D. Received	Cash	Bank

Unit 2

FINANCIAL STATEMENTS

Income Statement

It is a financial statement used to determine the performance of a business in terms of profits or losses.

Format

DCE TRADERS

INCOME STATEMENT

FOR THE YEAR ENDED 31/12/13

	$	$	$
Sales		xxx	
Less. Sales returns (Return inwards)		(xx)	xxx
Less. Cost of goods			
Opening inventory		xx	
Add. Purchases	xxx		
Carriage inwards	xx		
Less. Return outwards	(xx)	xxx	
		xxx	
Less. Closing inventory		(xx)	xxx
Gross profit			**xxx**
Add. Discount Received			xx
Commission income			xxx
Total income			**xxx**
Expenses			
Wages		xx	
Rent		xx	
Carriage outwards		xx	
Discount allowed		xx	
Electricity		xx	(xxx)
Net profit			**xxx**

Balance sheet/Statement of financial position

It is a financial statement that is used to determine the position of a business in terms of assets, liabilities and capital.

It applies the Accounting equation; A = C + L

Format

DCE TRADERS

BALANCE SHEET

AS AT 31/12/13

	$	$	$
Non-current assets			
Premises		xxx	
Furniture		xxx	
Motor vehicle		xxx	xxx
Current assets			
Inventory (closing)	xxx		
Accounts receivable	xxx		
Debtors	xxx		
Cash	xxx		
Bank	xxx	xxx	
Less. Current liabilities			
Accounts payable	xxx		
Overdraft	xxx	(xxx)	xxx
			xxx
Financed by			
Capital			xxx
Add. Net profit.			xxx
Less. Drawings.			xxx
			xxx

Example

The following balances were extracted from the books of Rose Baraka as at 31st March 2013:

Purchases $ 56,000

Carriage inwards $ 500

Sales $ 92,720

Return inwards $ 960

Return outwards $ 540

Salary and wages $ 14,640

Furniture $ 1,640

Accounts receivable $ 13,600

Accounts payable $ 15,800

Motor vehicle $ 14,000

Rent $ 4,200

Bank balance $ 7,900

Cash in hand $ 520

Discount Allowed $ 1,160

Discount received $ 740

Equipment $ 2,400

Sundry expenses $ 350

Inventory as at 1st April 2012. $ 7,680

Motor vehicle expenses $ 1,630

Capital as at 1st April 2012. $ 28,780

Drawings $ 11,400

Additional information:

Inventory as at 31st March 2013 was valued at $ 10,320,000.

Required

a) Prepare a Trial balance as at 31st March 2013.
b) Income statement for the year ended 31st March 2013.
c) Statement of financial position as at 31st March 2013.

Solution:

Rose Baraka   Trial Balance as at 31/03/13

Particulars	Dr.	Cr.
Capital		28,780
Purchases	56,000	
Sales		92,720
Carriage inwards	500	
Returns inward	960	
Returns outward		540
Wages	14,640	
Rent	4,200	
Motor vehicle	14,000	
Furniture	1,640	
Accounts receivable	13,600	
Accounts payable		15,800
Bank	7,800	
Cash in hand	520	
Discount allowed	1,160	
Discount received		740
Equipment	2,400	
Sundry expenses	350	
Drawings	11,400	
Motor vehicles expenses	1,630	
Inventory	7,680	
	138,500	**138,500**

Rose Baraka   Income Statement

	$	$	$
Sales		92,720	
Less. Returns inward		(960)	91,760
Cost of sales			
Opening inventory		7,680	
Purchases	56,000		
Less. Returns outward	(540)		
Add. Carriage inwards	500	55,960	
Goods available for sale		63,640	
Less. Closing stock		(10,320)	(53,320)
Gross profit			**38,440**
Add. Discount received			740
Total income			39,180
Expenses			
Salaries and wages		14,640	
Rent		4,200	
Discount allowed		1,160	
Sundry expenses		350	
Motor vehicle expenses		1,630	(21,980)
Net profit			**17,200**

Rose Baraka

Statement of financial position as at 31/03/13

	$	$	$
Non-current assets			
Furniture		1, 640	
Motor vehicle		14, 000	
Equipment		2, 400	18, 040
Current assets			
Inventory (closing)	10, 320		
Accounts receivable	13, 600		
Bank	7, 900		
Cash in hand	520	32, 340	
Less. Current liabilities			
Accounts payable		(15, 800)	16, 540
			34, 580
Financed by;			
Capital			28, 780
Add. Net profit			17, 280
Less. Drawings			(11, 400)
			34, 580

Adjustments to financial statements

1. *Accruals*

These are expenses or income but not paid.

a) **Accrued expense** are expenses incurred but not yet paid as at the end of the year.

The Accruals concept states; **expenses are recognized when incurred and not when paid. Therefore, the accrued expenses are added to expenses paid in the income statement.**

In the statement of financial position they are recognized as current liabilities. To recognize an accrued expense, debit expense account and credit accrued expense account.

Illustration:

Wages paid during the year ended 31st December, 2013 amounted to $ 180,000. However 20000 was still outstanding as at the end of the year.

Required: Wages expense account

Accrued expense account

Solution:

Dr.		Wages a/c				Cr
		$				$
31/12/13	Bank	180,000				
31/12/13	Accrued	20,000	31/12/13	Balance c/f		200,000
		200,000				**200,000**

Dr.		Accrued expense a/c				Cr.
		$				$
31/12/13	Balance c/f	**200,000**	31/12/13	Wages		**200,000**

b) **Accrued income** are incomes earned but not yet received.

The Accruals concept requires that incomes be recognized when earned and not when cash has been received.

To recognize accrued incomes debit Accrued income account and credit Income account.

The accrued incomes are added to the incomes received in the income statement and recognized as current assets in the statement of financial position.

Illustration:

Income earned during the year ended 31st December 2013 amounted to $ 300,000. However, only 250,000 have been received at the end of the year.

Prepare; i) Commission income account.

ii) Accrued commission account.

Solution:

Dr.		Commission income a/c				Cr.
		$				$
			31/12/13	Bank		250,000
31/12/13	Balance c/f	300,000	31/12/13	Accrued		50,000
		300,000				**300,000**

Dr.		Accrued commission a/c				Cr.
		$				$
31/12/13	Commission	**50,000**	31/12/13	Balance c/f		**50,000**

2. Prepayments

These are payments in advance.

I. Prepaid expenses

These are expenses paid in advance. They don't relate to the current year.

When preparing the final books of accounts only expenses for the current year are recognized. Therefore, any expenses paid in advance must be deducted from amounts paid.

To record prepaid expenses, debit prepaid expense account and credit expense account. Prepaid expenses are recognized as current assets in the statement of financial position.

Illustration:

Rent paid in the year ended 31st December 2013 amounted to $ 400,000. However, $ 50,000 relates to the year 2014.

Required: i) Rent expense account.

       ii) Prepaid rent account.

Solution:

Dr.		Rent expense a/c				Cr.
		$				$
31/12/13	Bank	400,000	31/12/13	Prepaid	50,000
			31/12/13	Balance c/f	350,000
		400,000			**400,000**

Dr.		Prepaid rent a/c				Cr.
		$				$
31/12/13	Rent	**50,000**	31/12/13	Balance c/f	**50,000**

II. Prepaid incomes are incomes received in advance before they are earned.

They are not supposed to be recognized as incomes for the year because they do not relate to the current year. They are therefore deducted from incomes received.

In the statement of financial position prepaid incomes are current liabilities. Double entry for prepaid income; debit income account and credit prepaid income account.

Illustration:

Commission received during the year ended 31st December 2013 amounted to $500,000.

$60,000 relate to January 2014. Prepare:

  a. Commission income account.
  b. Prepaid commission account.

Solution

Dr.	Commission income a/c				Cr.
		$			$
31/12/13	Prepaid	60,000	31/12/13	Bank	500,000
31/12/13	Balance c/f	440,000			
		500,000			**500,000**

Dr.	Prepaid commission a/c				Cr.
		$			$
31/12/13	Balance c/f	**60,000**	31/12/13	Commission	**60,000**

3. Bad debts
    - When a business sells Goods on credit they expect that debtors repay their debts. However, some debtors default payments resulting to Bad debts.
    - If as at the end of the year, the debtors will not have paid their debt they are eliminated from the books and I referred to as bad debts written off.
    - Both bad debts and bad debts written off are recognized as expenses in the income statement and are deducted from debtors in the statement of financial position. Double entry to recognize bad debts; debit bad debts/bad debts written off account and credit debtors account.

4. Provision for bad and doubtful debts

It is an estimate of debtors who are likely to default payment.

The provision is made in consistency with the prudence concepts which states; an estimate of all possible expenses and liabilities should be made during the year so that the performance and position of a business is not overstated.

To recognize provision for bad and doubtful debts, the following are considered:

When making provision for the first time debit income statement (expense) and credit provision for doubtful debts account.

In subsequent years consider increase or decrease in provision for bad and doubtful debts.

  i.   An **increase** is treated as an **expense** and recorded as; **debit** income statement and **credit** provision for doubtful debts account.
  ii. **Decrease** in a provision for bad and doubtful debts is treated as an **income** and is recorded as; **debit** provision for bad and doubtful debts account and **credit** income statement.

N/B: provision for bad and doubtful debts is computed as a percentage of debtors not of bad and doubtful debts.

Illustration:

Consider the following information on debtors:

Year	Debtors	Bad debts	Provision for doubtful debts
2011	2,500,000	20,000	2%
2012	2,800,000	10,000	2%
2013	2,600,000	15,000	2%

For each of the years ended 31st December 2011, 2012 and 2013. Prepare:

  i.   Debtors account
  ii. Bad debts account
  iii. Provision for bad and doubtful debts account.

Solution:

Dr.		Debtors a/c				Cr.
		$				$
1/01/11	Sales	2,500,000	31/12/11	Bad debts		20,000
			31/12/11	Balance c/f		2,480,000
		2,500,000				2,500,000
1/01/12	Sales	2,800,000	31/12/12	Bad debts		10,000
			31/12/12	Balance c/f		2,790,000
		2,800,000				2,800,000
1/01/13	Sales	2,600,000	31/12/13	Bad debts		15,000
			31/12/13	Balance c/f		2,585,000
		2,600,000				2,600,000

Dr.		Bad debts a/c			Cr.
		$			$
31/12/11	Debtors	20,000	31/12/11	Balance c/f	20,000
31/12/12	Debtors	10,000	31/12/12	Balance c/f	10,000
31/12/13	Debtors	15,000	31/12/13	Balance c/f	15,000

Provision for doubtful debts = % (Debtors - Bad debts)

Year 2011 = 2% (2,500,000 - 20,000) = 49,600

Year 2012 = 2% (2,800,000 - 10,000) = 55,800

Year 2013 = 2% (2,600,000 - 15,000) = 51,700

Note

An increase in provision for doubtful debts is recorded on the credit side of the provision for doubtful debts account while a decrease is recorded on the debit side. The increase/decrease is recorded in the income statement/profit and loss account.

Dr.	Provision for bad debts a/c					Cr.
		$				$
31/12/11	Balance c/f	**49,600**	31/12/11	Income statement		**49,600**
			1/01/12	Balance b/f		49,600
31/12/12	Balance c/f	55,800	31/12/12	Income statement		6,200
		55,800				**55,800**
31/12/13	Income statement	4,100	1/01/13	Balance b/f		55,800
31/12/13	Balance c/f	51,700				
		55,800				**55,800**

Unit 3

DEPRECIATION

What is depreciation?

It is the loss in value of tangible Non current assets.

Causes of depreciation

I.   Usage – When an acid is put into constant usage it tends to lose value.
II. Time – Assets lose value due to passage of time, even when not in use.
III. Changes in technology – This cause assets to become obsolete as better assets come up.
IV. Economic factors – This include expansion of the business causing inadequacy of assets.

Characteristics of depreciable assets

- Their cost must be capital in nature, i.e they must have been financed using capital.
- They must have been acquired for revenue generation or cost reduction.
- They should be tangible in nature.
- They must be useful to the business for a period of more than one year.

Reasons for accounting for depreciation

- To determine the real value of an asset. (Cost – Accumulated depreciation)
- Depreciation is used in the determination of profits.
- To be consistent with the matching concept which requires all expenses be deducted from corresponding incomes.
- To prevent consumption of capital.
- To be consistent with the prudence concept which states; the business should anticipate and recognize all the possible expenses and losses.
- For replacement purposes.

Terms used in depreciation

1. *Estimated useful life* – It is the number of years unless it is expected to be in use to the business.
2. *Salvage value/ residual value/ scrap value* – It is the value an asset is likely to fetch in the market after its estimated useful life.
3. *Depreciable amount* – It is the total loss in value of an asset over its estimated useful life.
4. *Annual depreciation* – It is the loss in value of an asset over a year.
5. *Accumulated depreciation/ provision for depreciation* – It is the total loss in value

of an asset at the end of a particular year.
6. *Net Book value/ written down value* – It is the value of an asset **net** of the provision for depreciation.

Methods for calculating depreciation

a) *Straight line method*

Depreciation of an asset remains constant over the estimated useful life. Is computed as follows;

- Given the cost of an asset, the estimated useful life and scrap value of an asset

$$\text{Annual depreciation} = \frac{\text{Cost - Scrap value}}{\text{Estimated useful life}}$$

- Given the cost and the estimated useful life

$$\text{Annual depreciation} = \frac{\text{Cost}}{\text{Estimated useful life}}$$

- Given the cost and the rate of depreciation
Annual depreciation = Rate × Cost

Illustration:

Vehicle with an estimated useful life of four years was acquired on 1st January 2013 for 1.2 million dollars, it is expected to have a scrap value of $200,000. Calculate the annual depreciation.

$$\text{Annual depreciation} = \frac{1,200,000 - 200,000}{4} = \$\ 250,000$$

Assuming the motor vehicle did not have a scrap value.

$$\text{Annual depreciation} = \frac{1,200,000}{4} = \$\ 300,000$$

Assuming the motor vehicle is depreciated at the rate of 10%.

Annual depreciation = 10% × 1,200,000 = $ 120,000

b) *Reducing balance method*

A uniform rate of depreciation is applied on the cost or net value of an asset.

- On acquisition of an asset

  Annual depreciation = Rate × Cost

- In subsequent years

  Annual depreciation = Rate × Net Book Value

Where Net Book Value = Cost − accumulated depreciation.

Illustration

Machinery costing $800,000 were acquired on 1st January 2010. The machines are depreciated at the rate of 10% per annum on written down value. Calculate annual depreciation of the machines for the next five years.

Solution

Machinery

Cost.	800,000
Annual depreciation 2010 (10% × 800,000)	(80,000)
Net Book value 2010	720,000
Annual depreciation 2011 (10% × 720,000)	(72,000)
Net Book value 2011	648,000
Annual depreciation 2012 (10% × 648,000)	(64,800)
Net Book value 2012	583,200
Annual depreciation 2013 (10% × 583,000)	(58,320)
Net Book value 2013	524,880
Annual depreciation 2014 (10% × 524,880)	(52,488)
Net Book value 2014	**472,392**

c) *Sum of digits method*

Depreciation is calculated as a proportion of the remaining estimated useful life of an asset at the beginning of a particular year and the total of the estimated useful life for the years an asset is expected to be used which is multiplied by the cost of the asset.

Illustration

Motor vehicle costing $1,000,000 was acquired on 1ˢᵗ January 2010. It has an estimated useful life of four years. Calculate annual depreciation for each of the four years using the sum of digits method.

Solution

Year	Remaining estimated useful life	Annual depreciation
2010	4	$\frac{4}{10} \times 1,000,000 = 400,000$
2011	3	$\frac{3}{10} \times 1,000,000 = 300,000$
2012	2	$\frac{2}{10} \times 1,000,000 = 200,000$
2013	1	$\frac{1}{10} \times 1,000,000 = 100,000$
	10	

Accounting for depreciation

Depreciation is recognized as an expense in the income statement and the double entry is; debit income statement and credit provision for depreciation.

Depreciation is usually accounted for in three accounts:

- Asset account
- Provision for depreciation account
- Disposal account

Disposal of assets

When an asset is disposed during the year the following adjustments are made;

- With the cost of the asset disposed; debit disposal account and credit asset account
- With the provision for depreciation of the asset up to the date of disposal; debit provision for depreciation account and credit disposal account.
- With the proceeds from disposal; debit cash or bank account and credit disposal account.
- The balancing figure in the disposal account is either a gain or a loss in disposal.

With a gain in disposal; debit disposal account and credit income statement.

With a loss in disposal; debit the income statement and credit disposal account.

Illustration

A machine which was acquired on 1st January 2010 for $500,000 was disposed on 1st January 2013 for $300,000. Depreciation is provided at the rate of 10% per annum on cost. Prepare a disposal account.

Solution

Date of purchase 1 January 2010	Cost = 500,000
Date of disposal 1 January 2013	Proceeds = 300,000
No. of years used = 3 years	Provision for depreciation = (10% × 500,000 × 3)
	= $ 150,000

Note

A loss on disposal is recorded on the credit side while a gain on disposal is recorded on the debit side.

Dr.		Disposal a/c			Cr.
		$			$
1/01/13	Machinery (cost)	500,000	1/01/13 Prov. for depreciation	150,000
			1/01/13 Cash/Bank	300,000
			1/01/13 Loss.	50,000
		500,000		500,000

Depreciation and time factor

When an asset is acquired or disposed during the year, the following methods are used to apportion depreciation;

Full year method

Under this, a full year depreciation is provided in the year of purchase and no depreciation is provided in the year of disposal.

Pro rata method

Under this, depreciation is apportioned to the number of months to acid is used in the year of purchase and disposal.

Illustration

A motor vehicle costing $800,000 was acquired on 1st April 2012. It was disposed on 1st June 2013 for $600,000. Depreciation is provided at the rate of 15% per annum on costs. Prepare a disposal account assuming:

   a. Full year method
   b. Pro rata method

Solution

Full year method

15% × 800,000 = 120,000

Dr.		Disposal a/c			Cr.
		$			$
1/06/13	Motor vehicle	800,000	1/06/13 Prov. for depreciation		120,000
			1/06/13 Cash/Bank		600,000
			1/06/13 Loss		80,000
		800,000			**800,000**

Pro-rata method

Depreciation in the year of purchase = $\frac{9}{12}$ × 800,000 × 15% = 90,000

Depreciation in the year of disposal = $\frac{5}{12}$ × 800,000 × 15% = 50,000

Total provision for depreciation = 90,000 + 50,000 = $ 140,000

Dr.		Disposal a/c			Cr
		$			$
1/06/13	Motor vehicle	800,000	1/06/13 Prov. for depreciation		140,000
			1/06/13 Cash/Bank		600,000
			1/06/13 Loss		60,000
		800,000			**800,000**

Unit 4

CONTROL ACCOUNTS

What is a control account?

This is an account prepared to determine arithmetic accuracy of a Ledger account specifically the debtors Ledger account and creditors Ledger account.

Purpose

- Detection and correction of errors in the Ledger account.
- Determination of debtors and creditors balances for use in the final accounts.
- They are used as a tool of internal control over debtors and creditors to prevent occurrence of fraud.
- Speeds up preparation of final accounts.
- Apps to separate the duties between the accountant responsible for Ledgers and another for control accounts.

Note:

A contra settlement occurs when a customer is both a supplier and a purchaser, and it is recorded as; Debit purchase ledger control account and Credit sales ledger control account

Contra settlements are also referred to as **set offs.**

Sales leger control account

It is a control account which summarizes entries and balances of all individual accounts of customers in the sales ledger.

It is also known as total debtors account.

Sources of information in sales ledger control account

i. Opening balance on the closing balances are obtained from the schedule of debtors.
ii. Credit sales are obtained from sales day book.
iii. Receipts from debtors are obtained from the bank column of the cash book.
iv. Discount allowed obtained from the cash book.
v. Returns inwards are obtained from the returns inwards day book.

Format

Sales ledger control account

Dr.				Cr.
Balance b/f	xxx	Balance b/f		xxx
Credit sales	xxx	Returns inward		xxx
Debtors dishonored cheques	xxx	Bad debts written off		xxx
Interest on overdue a/c	xxx	Discount allowed		xxx
		Set offs		xxx
		Receipts from debtors		xxx
Balance c/f	xxx	Balance c/f		xxx
	xxx			**xxx**

Purchase ledger control account

It is a control account which summarizes the entries and balances of all individual accounts of suppliers in the purchases Ledger.

It is also known as total creditors account

Sources of information in purchase ledger control account

i.   Opening and closing balances from the schedule of creditors.
ii. Credit purchases are obtained from the purchases day book.
iii. Payments to creditors are obtained from the cash book.
iv. Discount received is obtained from the cash book.
v.   Returns outwards are obtained from returns outwards day book.

Format

Purchase ledger control account

Dr.			Cr.
Balance b/f	xxx	Balance b/f	xxx
Payments to creditors	xxx	Credit purchases	xxx
Returns outward	xxx	Interest on creditors overdue a/c	xxx
Discount received	xxx	Creditors dishonored cheques	xxx
Set offs	xxx		
Balance c/f	xxx	Balance c/f	xxx
	xxx		**xxx**

Bank Reconciliation statement

It is a statement prepared to account for the difference between the cash book Bank column and the bank statement.

When money is received it is debited in the cash book and when deposited to the bank account it is credited in the bank statement.

Payments are credited in the cash book but debited to the bank statement.

If all transactions are recorded, the balances in the cash book and bank statement must be equal and opposite. However, this is not always the case and it is therefore necessary to prepare a bank reconciliation statement.

Causes of difference between the cash book and bank statement

I.   *Items appearing in the cash book but missing in the bank statement*

They include;

a) Uncredited checks

These are checks received from debtors and debited in the cash book but not yet credited by the bank in the account as at the end of the year.

b) Un presented checks

These are checks paid out by the business but the recipients haven't presented them to the bank for payment.

c) Over banking and/or short banking

These are errors that arises when recording items in the bank statement. They lead to overstating or understating bank balances.

II.   *Items appearing in the bank statement but missing in the cash book*

They include;

a) Bank charges

These are fees charged by the bank for maintaining the account and executing transactions.

b) Standing orders

These are instructions to the bank to execute payment on behalf of the account holder. For example, loan repayments, insurance premiums, etc.

c) Direct credits

This is where the bank has recorded a receipt of cash but the business is unaware of the payment and will therefore not have recorded the receipt in the cash book.

d) Dishonored or unpaid checks

These are checks paid to or out of the business account but which are either stopped by the drawer or returned by the owner.

e) Transfers

Is the transfer of money from one account to another

f) Direct debits

These are payments made directly from the business account.

Format

Updated cash book

Dr.				Cr.
	$			$
Balance b/f	xxx	Bank charges		xxx
Transfers into the a/c	xxx	Standing orders		xxx
Direct credits	xxx	Direct debits		xxx
Errors understating cash book bal.	xxx	Dishonored cheques		xxx
		Transfers from the a/c		xxx
		Errors overstating cash book bal.	xxx
	___	Balance c/f		xxx
	xxx			**xxx**

Bank Reconciliation statement

	$
Balance as per updated cash book	xxx
Add. Unpresented cheques	xxx
Over bankings	xxx
Less. Uncredited cheques	(xxx)
Short bankings	(xxx)
	___
Balance as per bank statement	**xxx**

Trade in

It is the exchange of an asset for another asset. At the time of exchange the owner of the old asset present the asset to the seller of the new asset at an agreed price known as **trade in value.**

To get the new asset an additional amount of money is paid by the buyer this is known as **cash consideration**.

To get the value of the new asset;

Value of the new assets = Trade in value + Cash consideration

At the time of trade in, the old asset is treated as a disposal and the trade in value is the proceeds from disposal. While the new asset is treated as a purchase and is recognized in the books at cost.

Insurance compensation

Sometimes occurrences such as accidents, fires, flood, etc. may arise destroying assets of a business. In case the business had insured its assets against such occurrences, the insurance company will compensate the business of the assets destroyed.

When an asset is destroyed, it is treated as though it has been disposed and insurance compensation is proceeds from disposal.

Revaluation of assets

It is the change of value of an asset to make it consistent to the market values. This is especially so when the cost of the asset differs significantly with the market value such that recognizing the asset at historical cost will be misleading. Revaluation can either be upwards or downwards. An upward revaluation arises when the revalued amount of an asset is greater than the cost or Net Book value. An upwards revaluation results to a revaluation Surplus which is recognized as;

Debit asset account and Credit revaluation reserved.

Revaluation reserved is recognized in the statement of financial position under capital and liabilities.

A downwards revaluation arises when the revalued amount is less than the cost or net Book value of the asset. It results to a revaluation loss which is recorded as;

Debit revaluation reserved account (income statement) and credit asset account.

When an asset is revalued the provision for depreciation up to the date of Revaluation is written as follows;

Debit provision for depreciation account and credit asset account.

There after, the asset is depreciated over the remaining estimated useful life.

IAS 16, Property, Plant and Equipment Movement Schedule

It is a schedule that shows the movement of assets during the year in terms of acquisition, disposal, revaluation, reclassification and depreciation.

Format

	Land & buildings	Plant & machinery	Motor vehicle	Total
Balance b/f cost on 1 Jan	xxx	xxx	xxx	xxx
Add. Acquisitions	xxx	xxx	xxx	xxx
Revaluation(surplus/loss)	xx/(xx)	xx/(xx)	xx/(xx)	xxx
Less disposal	(xx)	(xx)	(xx)	(xxx)
Less fully depreciated assets	(xx)	(xx)	(xx)	(xxx)
Depreciation on revaluation	(xx)	(xx)	(xx)	(xxx)
A. Balance c/f as at 31 Dec	**xxx**	**xxx**	**xxx**	**xxx**
Balance b/f Prov. for depreciation	xxx	xxx	xxx	xxx
Less disposal	(xx)	(xx)	(xx)	(xx)

Less depreciation on revaluation	(xx)	(xx)	(xx)	(xx)
Less depreciation on fully depreciated assets	(xx)	(xx)	(xx)	(xx)
Add depreciation for the year	xxx	xxx	xxx	xxx
B. Balance c/f prov. for depreciation	**xxx**	**xxx**	**xxx**	**xxx**
C. Net Book Value (**A – B**)	**xxx**	**xxx**	**xxx**	**xxx**

Accounting for non-profit making organizations

These are organizations established for other purposes other than Trading especially to bring together members of common interests.

Sources of income

- **Members subscriptions** – Are contributions made by members on annual basis to retain membership. To determine subscriptions for the year, a subscriptions account is prepared.

  Subscriptions in arrears are those due but not yet received as at the end of the year. They are recognized as **current assets** in the statement of financial position.

  Subscriptions in advance are those received before their due dates. They are recognized as **current liabilities** in the statement of financial position.

- **Income from trading** – Some organizations carry out trading activities to ensure welfare of members. For such trading activities an income statement is prepared and the profit or loss is recognized in the income and expenditure account.
- **Incomes from social activities** – These include tournaments, dinners and other forms of competition. Entrance fees from such events is recognized as an income in the income and expenditure account.
- **Investment income** – This include; shares from listed and unlisted companies, treasury bills, bonds, etc. Their income may be in form of dividend or interest.
- **Donations** – Are contributions from well wishers. There are two types of donations;   a) *Specific donation*

It is a contribution in a specific project in mind. Specific donations are not recognized as incomes, instead they are recorded in the specific project fund and recognized in the statement of financial position.

b) *General donations*

These are donations without a specific project in mind. They are recognized as incomes in the Income and expenditure account.

- **Life membership fees** – These are contributions by members who wish to enjoy benefits of the club or society for a lifetime. The lump sum amount contributed is spread over the number of years one is expected to enjoy the benefits.

Final Accounts

a) Receipts and payments account

It is an equivalent of a cash book on trading organizations. It has the following features;

i. It is prepared on cash basis, i.e it records only cash received and cash paid.
ii. It is debited with receipts and credited with payments.
iii. The opening balance represents the cash or bank balance at the beginning of the year while the closing balance represents the cash or bank balance at the end of year.

b) Income and Expenditure account

It is an equivalent of the income statement. It has the following features;

i. It is prepared on accrual basis, i.e it records both cash and credit transactions.
ii. The excess of income over expenditure represents a **surplus** while the excess of expenditure over income represents a **deficit**.

Unit 5

PARTNERSHIP

It is a form of business organization that involves multiple ownership. Two or more persons may form a partnership to carry out business in common with a view of making profit.

Nature of partnership

- Partnership will be formed with a minimum of two persons and a maximum of twenty.
- Any association of more than 20 and less than 50 people carrying on business in common with a view to profit is required to register as a private limited liability company. But they may also opt to register as a public company.

Partnership Deeds/ Agreements

This is a document that defines the relationship between the partnership. A partnership deed/agreement may be in writing (documented) or implied. It is always better if the agreement is documented.

Where the agreement is documented it should address the following;

   I.   Amount of capital to be contributed by each partner.
  II.   The ratio in which loss or profits should be shared.
 III.   Whether partners should receive interest on capital.
 IV.   Whether partners should be charged interest on drawings.
  V.   Whether partners should are entitled to salaries and commissions and the method of computation.
 VI.   The process of admission of a new partner.
VII.   The process to be followed on retirement or death of a partner.

Rights of a partner

   I.   *Right to access to accounts* – Every partner has a right to have access to and inspect any books of the firm.
  II.   *Right to be consulted in case of dispute of management* – Every partner has the right to be consulted in all matters affecting the business of the partnership before any decision is made by the partners.
 III.   *Right to share in profit* – All partners are entitled to share equally in the capital and profits and must contribute equally to losses whether of capital or otherwise.
 IV.   *Right to interest on capital* – The partnership agreement may contain a clause as to the right of the partners to claim interest on capital at a certain rate, usually 5% per annum.

Partnership Account

The following additional accounts will be necessary in a partnership environment;

I. Profit and loss appropriation account
II. Partners capital account
III. Partners current account

Appropriation account is prepared to show the distribution of profits between partners.

Current account is maintained to record transactions between partners and the partnership. Where current accounts are maintained, the partners capital are fixed (*to ensure that partners don't draw more money than profit earned*).

Example

Robert and John are in partnership, sharing profits and losses in the ratio 3:2 respectively. After crediting their account with interest on capital 10% per annum, and monthly salaries of $15,000 and $20,000 respectively. Interest on drawings is charged at 5% per annum. The trial balance as at 31st December 2012 after drawing profit and loss account is as follows:

	$	$
Capital		
Robert		500,000
John		400,000
Current a/c		
Robert		20,000
John		10,000
Drawings		
Robert	225,000	
John	215,000	
Net profit		800,000
Fixed assets (cost)		
Land & buildings	500,000	
Plant & machinery	300,000	
Motor vehicle	200,000	
Accumulated depreciation		
Land & buildings		100,000
Plant & machinery		50,000
Motor vehicle		50,000
Debtors	100,000	
Stock	200,000	
Cash	290,000	
Creditors		
	2,030,000	**2,030,000**

Required:

a) *Draw profit and loss appropriation account.*
b) *Partners current account.*
c) *Balance sheet as at 31st December 2012.*

Solution:

Robert and John profit and loss appropriation a/c

For the year ended 31/12/2012

Net profit			800,000
Interest on drawings			
Robert			11,250
John			10,750
			822,000
Interest on capital			
Robert		50,000	
John		40,000	
Salaries			
Robert		180,000	
John		240,000	(510,000)
			312,000
Share of profit			
Robert	187,200		
John	124,800		

Dr.	Robert current a/c			Cr.
Interest on drawings	11,250	Balance b/f	20,000
Drawings	225,000	Salaries	180,000
		Interest on capital	50,000
Balance c/f	200,950	Share of profit	187,200
	437,200		**437,200**

Dr.	John current a/c			Cr.
Interest on drawings	10,750	Balance b/f	10,000
Drawings	215,000	Salaries	240,000
		Interest on capital	40,000
Balance c/f	189,050	Share of profit	124,800
	414,800		**414,800**

Robert and John partnership

Balance sheet as at 31/12/2012

Non-current assets			
Motor vehicle	200,000	50,000	150,000
Plant & machinery	300,000	50,000	250,000
Land & buildings	500,000	100,000	400,000
			800,000
Current assets			
Stock	200,000		
Cash	290,000		
Debtors	100,000	590,000	
Current liabilities			
Creditors		(100,000)	490,000
			1,290,000
Financed by;			
Capital			
Robert		500,000	
John		400,000	
Current a/c			
Robert		200,950	
John		189,050	
			1,290,000

COMPANY ACCOUNT

A company is a body corporate governed by The Company's Act.

Types of companies

a) **Private company** – Owned by a minimum of 2 and a maximum of 50 members. Any transfer of shares is restricted and has to be approved by board of directors.

b) **Public limited company** – Owned by a minimum of 7 and no specified maximum members. Shares are freely transferable and expansion of the company can be achieved through the sale of shares to the public.

Classes of capital

Capital of a limited company is divided into shares which are allotted to members for cash or other assets transferred by them to the company.

I.*Registered/Authorized capital*

It is the maximum amount of capital the company expects to raise from its shares and is stated in the Memorandum of Association.

II.*Issued capital*

Out of the company's capital authorized, the directors may decide to put some of it to the public so as to start subscribing for and the company begins with.

III.*Called up capital*

Once the shares have been put to the public so as to start applying for, then the shareholders are called upon to subscribe or pay.

IV.*Paid up capital*

It is the actual amount received from the subscribers by the company out of the called up capital. The amount **unpaid** is known as **called in arrears**.

The final accounts of a limited company constitutes;

    a) Trading account
    b) Profit and Loss account
    c) Appropriation of profit and loss account
    d) Balance sheet

Profit and loss account

The following will be debited in a limited company;

    • Directors' salaries (fees)
    • Debentures interest
    • Auditors fee

Appropriation account

A limited company is supposed to pay tax on its profits which is known as corporate tax.

The profits distributed among the shareholders are known as dividends. They may be of two types, i.e ordinary or preference dividends. A limited company also transfers some amounts to general reserves.

All these are appropriation of profits and are to be debited to the appropriation section.

- Corporate tax and proposed dividends appear as current liabilities in the balance sheet.
- Amount transferred to general reserves is credited to the general reserves account.
- Profit and loss balance c/f is shown as a separate figure in the balance sheet.

Format

APPROPRIATION OF PROFIT AND LOSS A/C

Dr.				Cr.
		$		$
Corporation tax		xx	Net profit	xx
Transfers to general reserves		xx	Profit and loss a/c b/f	xx
Dividends				
Paid	xx			
Proposed	xx			
Profit and loss a/c c/f	xx	xx		____
		xxx		**xxx**

Balance sheet

- All capitals are shown separately, i.e preference shares, ordinary shares, etc.
- Companies are required to show the cost of fixed assets, accumulated depreciation is deducted to get the Net Book Value.
- Investments of a limited company are shown as an asset and appear between fixed assets and current assets.

Format

BALANCE SHEET AS AT ****

Dr.   Cr.

Fixed assets	Cost	Depr.	NBV	Authorized share capital		
Plant & machinery	xx	xx	xx	Ordinary share capital $10 each		
Furniture	xx	xx	xx	Issued share capital		
Motor vehicle	xx	xx	xx	10,000 ordinary shares $10 each 100,000		
	xx	**xx**	xx	Share premium		xxx
				General reserves		xxx
Investment			xx	Profit & loss a/c		xxx
Current assets				10% debentures		xxx
Stock		xx		Current liabilities		
Debtors		xx		Creditors	xx	
Bank		xx		Proposed dividends	xx	
Cash		xx	xxx	Corporate tax	xx	xxx
			xxx			**xxx**

MANUFACTURING ACCOUNTS

These are accounts prepared by those business in the manufacturing industry.

Terms used in the manufacturing account

- **Direct cost** – Are cost that can be traced to the final product. They include; direct materials, labor and direct expenses. They are also known as *prime cost.*
- **Indirect cost** – Are costs that can't be traced to the final product. They include; factory rent, electricity, water, etc. They are also known as *production overheads.*
- **Work in progress** – These are units of production which are incomplete by the end of the year.
- **Finished goods** – Are items of production whose production process is complete by the end of the year and transferred to the warehouse awaiting sale.
- **Raw materials** – Are goods acquired for further processing.
- **Production cost** – Cost incurred to manufacture finished goods.

Production cost = Prime cost + Indirect cost/overheads + opening work in progress – closing work in progress.

- **Transfer price** – It arises when finished goods are transferred to the warehouse at a value different from the production cost.
- **Transfer profit** – It arises when the transfer price is higher than the production cost.

Transfer profit = Transfer price – Production cost

Transfer price/cost = Production cost + Transfer profit

- **Unrealized profit** – When goods are transferred to the warehouse at a transfer profit, it is expected that goods will be sold for the profit to be realized. However, at the end of the year some units may remain unsold resulting to unrealized profits.

Unrealized profit is recognized as an expense in the income statement in the year it first occurs. In subsequent years, consider increase or decrease in unrealized profits. An increase is treated as an expense while a decrease is treated as an income.

Format

ACB Manufacturing Income statement
For the year ended 31/12/10

	$	$
Opening stock (raw materials)		xxx
Purchases (raw materials)		xxx
Less. Closing stock (raw materials)		(xxx)
		xxx
Direct labor		xxx
Direct expenses		xxx
Prime cost		**xxx**
Production overheads		
Depreciation (plant & machinery)	xxx	
Factory rent	xxx	
Factory lighting & heating	xxx	xxx
		xxx
Add. Opening work in progress		xxx
Less. Closing work in progress		xxx
Production cost		**xxx**
Add. Transfer profit		xxx
Transfer price		**xxx**
Sales		xxx
Less. Cost of sales		
Opening stock	xxx	
Production cost/Transfer price	xxx	
	xxx	
Less. Closing stock	(xxx)	(xxx)
Gross profit		**xxx**
Add. Transfer profit		xxx
Other incomes		xxx
Total income		xxx
Expenses		
Administrative expenses (office rent, printing & stationery, etc)	xxx	
Selling & Distribution (Discount allowed, advertising, etc)	xxx	
Other costs (Interest on loan, loss on disposal, transfer loss, etc)	xxx	
Transfer loss	xxx	(xxx)
Net profit		**xxx**

	$	$
Non-current assets		N.B.V
Production equipment		xxx
Current assets		
Inventory - raw materials	xxx	
- work in progress	xxx	
- finished goods	xxx	
Trade receivables	<u>xxx</u>	<u>xxx</u>
		<u>xxx</u>
Financed by;		
Capital	xxx	
Add. Net profit	xxx	
Less. Drawings	(<u>xxx</u>)	xxx
Liabilities		
Loan	xxx	
Bank overdraft	xxx	
Trade payables	<u>xxx</u>	<u>xxx</u>
	<u>xxx</u>	**<u>xxx</u>**

STATEMENTS OF CASH FLOW

It is a financial statement prepared to determine availability of cash or cash equivalents in a business to finance liabilities when they fall due.

A business may report profits and still be unable to finance its debts due to the following reasons;

I. The income statement is prepared on accrual basis therefore the incomes may not have been received.
II. Acquisition of assets.
III. Payments of dividends and interests.
IV. Repayments of loans and redemption of preference shares.

Importance of cash flow statements

i. To assess the business ability to repay its debts when they fall due.
ii. To compare the business' performance with that of other businesses in the same industry and with the same assets.
iii. To determine the sources and uses of cash in a business.
iv. For trend analysis, i.e to compare performance of a business over a period of time in terms of liquidity.

Terms used in cash flow statements

- **Working capital changes** – This refers to increases or decreases in current assets and current liabilities such as stock, debtors, prepayments, accruals and trade payables.
- **Non-cash items** – Are expenses or incomes that don't results to changes in cash flow. For example, depreciation, impairment of Goodwill, amortization of intangible assets, loss or gain on disposal, etc.
- **Operating activities** – Are activities that results to generation of profit. They include; sales, purchases, payments for expenses, incomes.
- **Investing activities** – Are activities that results to acquisition or disposal of Non current assets and any income from the Non current assets such as investment income.
- **Financing activities** – this relates to activities that result to generation or usage of finances in a business. They include; issue of shares, redemption of shares, acquisition of loans, repayment of loans, payment of interest, dividends and premium issue of shares.
- **Cash and cash equivalents** – Are items that are either in form of cash or can be easily converted into cash. They include; cash in hand, cash at bank, marketable security, bank overdraft, etc.

Format

ACB LIMITED STATEMENT OF CASH FLOW FOR THE YEAR ENDED 31/12/12		
	$	$
Operating activities		
Profit before interest & tax	xxx	
Adjust for non-cash items		
Depreciation	xxx	
Loss on disposal	xxx	
Impairment	xxx	
Amortization	xxx	
Gain on disposal	(xxx)	
Cash flow before working capital changes	xxx	
Working capital changes		
Increase in current assets	(xxx)	
Decrease in current assets	xxx	
Increase in current liabilities	xxx	
Decrease in current liabilities	(xxx)	
Cash flow before tax	**xxx**	
Less. Tax paid	(xxx)	
Cash flow from operating activities		*xxx*
Investment activities		
Acquisition of non-current assets	(xxx)	
Disposal of non-current assets	xxx	
Investment income	xxx	
Cash flow from investing activities		*xxx*
Financing activities		
Issue of shares (cash)	xxx	
Premium on issue	xxx	
Redemption of shares	(xxx)	
Payment of dividends	(xxx)	
Payment of interest	(xxx)	
Acquisition of loans	xxx	
Repayment of loans	(xxx)	
Cash flow from financing activities		*XXX*
Total changes in cash flow		xxx
Add. Cash & cash equivalents b/f		xxx
Cash & cash equivalents c/f		**XXX**

RATIO ANALYSIS

What is ratio?

It is the indicated quotient of two mathematical expressions and the relationship between them.

A ratio can be expressed as a percentage, fraction or stated comparison between the numbers. The purpose of calculating the accounting ratio is to try to shed light on the financial progress or otherwise of a company by discovering trends and movements in the relationship between figures.

Ratio analysis therefore helps to analyze and interpret the overall performance stated in financial statements.

NOTE: Accounting officials are only a guide and cannot form the basis for financial conclusions. They only offer clues and point to factors requiring further investigation.

Types of Ratios

1. **Profitability Ratios**

Profitability ratio measures the overall performance and effectiveness of the firm. These ratios measure the company's profitability in relation to sales and investment. The following are the main profitability ratios;

- **Return on capital employed (R.O.C.E)**

This ratio shows how well funds are used to generate profits or income. It is also known as primary ratio and is calculated as;

$$R.O.C.E = \frac{\text{Net profit before interest and tax}}{\text{Capital employed}} \times 100$$

Capital employed = Fixed assets + Current assets − Current liabilities

Capital employed can also be arrived at by;

Capital employed = Share capital + Reserves + Long term debts

- **Gross profit margin**

This is the gross ratio which compares the gross profit and sales. The higher the gross profit margin the better since that portrays higher profitability.

It is arrived at by; $\frac{\text{Gross profit}}{\text{Sales}} \times 100$

- **Return on equity**

The higher the return on investment the better and vice versa. This is also referred to as the Return on investment. This ratio is given by;

$$\text{Return on equity} = \frac{\text{Earnings attributable to shareholders}}{\text{Net worth}} \times 100$$

Net worth = share capital + share premium + reserves + shareholders + surplus − losses

2. **Liquidity Ratios**

These ratios measure the businesses' ability to meet current financial obligations. Bad liquidity may result in poor credit worthiness and legal tangles hence businesses must ensure that they neither have excess liquidity nor inadequate liquidity.

The liquidity ratios include;

- **Current ratio**

This is also known as the working capital ratio. The ideal current ratio is 2:1, which means businesses or companies can pay off their current liabilities by liquidating current assets and still remain with cash to sustain their operations.

It measures the short-term solvency of a business or company. It is arrived at by;

$$\text{Current ratio} = \frac{\text{Current assets}}{\text{Current liabilities}}$$

- **Cash ratio**

It determines the cash and its equivalent to current liabilities. It is given by;

$$\text{Cash ratio} = \frac{\text{Cash + Marketable securities}}{\text{Current liabilities}}$$

- **Quick ratio**

It is also known as the **acid-test ratio**. The ideal ratio is 1:1. This ratio establishes the relationship between liquid assets and current liabilities. It is given by;

$$\text{Quick ratio} = \frac{\text{Current assets}}{\text{Current liabilities}} - \text{Stock}$$

Note: Stock is not a liquid asset since it requires time to be converted into cash.

3. *Efficiency Ratios*

These ratios are also known as turnover ratios / asset usage ratios or activity ratios. They measure the businesses' efficiency after employing available resources. An increase in these ratios indicates quick expansion while a decrease shows a fall in demand for the firm's products.

- ### *Debtors collection period*

It is the number of days, weeks or months the firm will take to collect money from its customers. It is given by;

$$\text{Debtors collection period} = \frac{\text{Debtors}}{\text{Credit sales}} \times 365 \text{ days}$$

It can also be arrived at by;

$$\frac{\text{Number of days/weeks or months in a year}}{\text{Debtors turnover}}$$

- ### *Rate of stock turnover*

It is also known as inventory turnover. It shows the number of times inventory is converted into sales. The higher the frequency of selling stock the better because a higher turnover is a better indicator since it means that the firm is efficient in selling its product. It is arrived at by;

$$\text{Inventory turnover} = \frac{\text{Cost of sales}}{\text{Average stock}}$$

$$\text{Average stock} = \frac{\text{Opening stock} + \text{Closing stock}}{2}$$

- ### *Debtors turnover*

It is the number of times debtors are converted into Cash. The higher the number, the more efficient is the firm. It is given by;

$$\text{Debtors turnover} = \frac{\text{Credit sales}}{\text{Debtors}}$$

- ### *Creditors turnover*

It is the number of times payment is made to suppliers. The shorter the number of times the better. It is arrived at by;

$$\text{Creditors turnover} = \frac{\text{Credit purchases}}{\text{Creditors}}$$

- **Total assets turnover**

It shows the relationship between sales and total assets. The higher the ratio the better. It is arrived at by;

$$\text{Total assets turnover} = \frac{\text{Sales}}{\text{Total assets}}$$

- **Creditors payment period**

It is the number of days, weeks or years the firm will take to make payments to suppliers. The longer the period the better. It is given by;

$$\text{Creditors payment period} = \frac{\text{Creditors}}{\text{Credit purchases}} \times 365 \text{ days}$$

- **Current assets turnover**

This shows the relationship between current assets and sales. The higher the ratio the better. It is given by;

$$\text{Current assets turnover} = \frac{\text{Sales}}{\text{Current assets}}$$

4. **Gearing Ratios**

These ratios are also known as the *debt or capital structure ratios*. They measure the firm's Financial Risk and its ability of utilizing debt capital to stockholders advantage. There should be an appropriate mix of debt and owner's equity in financing the firm's asset.

Financial leverage/Trading on equity – The process of magnifying the shareholder's return through employment of debt.

These ratios include;

- **Debt ratio**

It is given by;
$$\text{Debt ratio} = \frac{\text{Total liabilities}}{\text{Total assets}}$$

- *Interest cover*

It is given by;

$$\text{Interest cover} = \frac{\text{Profit before interest and tax}}{\text{Interest expense}}$$

- *Debt equity ratio*

It is given by;

$$\text{Debt equity ratio} = \frac{\text{Total debt}}{\text{Total equity}}$$

Total debt = Debentures + Preference share capital

- *Capital gearing ratio*

It is the debt to equity ratio. It is given by;

$$= \frac{\text{Preference share capital + Debentures}}{\text{Share capital + Reserves + Long-term debt}}$$

PRACTICE QUESTIONS

QUESTION ONE

The following are the summarized purchase and sales ledger transactions of Idambila Ltd for November 2015.

		$
1 November 2015	Purchase ledger balance	81,400
	Sales ledger balance	157,400
Transactions during November 2015:		
Cash purchases		4,700
Cash sales		19,300
Credit purchases		75,100
Credit sales		151,200
Returns outwards		1,100
Returns inward		2,200
Discounts allowed		1,700
Discounts received		2,400
Contras (set offs)		3,600
Bad debts written off		2,900
Customers dishonoured cheques		1,600
Receipts from debtors		146,100
Payments to creditors		74,800
Increase in provision for doubtful debts		1,900

Required:

a) Purchase ledger control account for the month ended 30 November 2015.
b) Sales ledger control account for the month ended 30 November 2015.
c) Explain the need for a Bank Reconciliation Statement.

QUESTION TWO

The following balances as at 29 February 2016 have been extracted from the accounting records of Golden Hen Ltd:

	$
Raw material in stock at 01/03/15	10,000
Raw material purchases	125,000
Carriage inwards	5,000
Direct labour	150,000
Indirect factory labour	80,000
Factory power (indirect)	30,000
Insurance of production equipment	10,000
Depreciation of production equipment	50,000
Other production overheads	40,000
Work in progress at 01/03/15	30,000
Finished goods stock at 01/03/15	50,000
Sales	760,000

Distribution costs	160,000
Administration expenses	140,000
Raw material in stock at 29/02/16	15,000
Work in progress at 29/02/16	35,000
Finished goods stock at 29/02/16	45,000

Required:
a) Prepare the manufacturing account for the year ended 29 February 2016.
b) Describe FIVE methods of providing for depreciation, illustrate with working examples.
c) Explain **apportionment of expenses**.

QUESTION THREE

The following trial balance has been taken from the books of Alexandra Ltd as at 29 February 2016:

	$	$
Turnover		2,050,000
Purchases	1,025,000	
Stock (inventory) (01 03 15)	165,000	
Postage and stationery	20,000	
Rent, rates and insurance	66,000	
Advertising	125,000	
Heating and lighting	90,000	
Auditor's fee	14,000	
Salaries	202,000	
Debenture interest	5,000	
Wages	141,000	
Creditors (amounts payable)		124,000
Provision for doubtful debts		20,000
Equipment at cost	710,000	
Depreciation of equip. (01 03 15)		110,000
Debentures (5%)		200,000
Ordinary share capital ($1)		100,000
Profit and loss a/c bal. (01 03 15)		160,000
Debtors (amounts receivable)	206,000	
Bank balance (overdrawn)		5,000
	2,769,000	2,769,000
	========	========

Additional information:
• Stock (inventory) 29 February 2016 is valued at $140,000
• Salaries owing amounted to $17,000
• Insurance prepaid amounted to $5,000
• The provision for doubtful debts is to be reduced to $15,000
• The equipment is to be depreciated by 40% on written down value
• The directors wish to provide $30,000 for corporation tax
• The directors have declared an ordinary dividend of 50p per share
Required:
a) Prepare the income statement (profit and loss account) for the year ended 29 February 2016.
b) Prepare the position statement (balance sheet) as at 29 February 2016.

QUESTION FOUR
The summarized financial statements of Lewis Ltd for 2015 and 2016 were as follows:
Lewis Ltd position statements (balance sheets) as at 29 February:

	2015 $000	$000	2016 £000	$000
Fixed assets at cost	25,000		40,000	
Depreciation	(15,000)	10,000	(26,000)	14,000
Current assets (non-fixed assets)				
Stock (inventory)	15,000		14,000	
Debtors (amounts receivable)	12,000		13,000	
Bank	1,000		3,000	
	28,000		30,000	
Current liabilities				
Creditors (amounts payable)	5,000		4,000	
Taxation	6,000		5,000	
Dividends	4,000		9,000	
	15,000		18,000	
Working capital		13,000		12,000
Long-term loans		(5,000)		
		18,000		26,000
Capital and reserves:				
Ordinary shares (£1)		10,000		10,000
Profit and loss account		10,000		16,000
		20,000		26,000

Lewis Ltd income statement (profit and loss account) for the year ended 29 February 2016:

	$000
Operating profit	20,200
Interest paid	(200)
Profit before tax	20,000
Taxation	(5,000)
Profit after tax	15,000
Dividend	(9,000)
Retained profit	6,000

Required:
a) Prepare a cash flow statement for Lewis Ltd for the year ended 29 February 2016.
b) Comment on the change in liquidity between the two balance sheets, credit will be given for the use of ratios and identification of sources of cash.

QUESTION FIVE
The following transactions need to be written up in a three column cash book:
01/02/16 Debit balances brought forward – bank £4,000 cash £500.
03/02/16 Paid rent £1,000 (cheque).
05/02/16 Received the following cheques: Axel £285, Bella £475 and Carlos £665.
All three debtors have ALREADY been allowed a 5% cash discount.
06/02/16 Cash sales £2,800.
09/02/16 Paid wages £1,000 (cash).

10/02/16 Paid cheques to the following suppliers: Robert £190, Mary £475 and William £570.
All three suppliers have ALREADY allowed a 5% cash discount.
13/02/16 Bought equipment £14,000 (cheque).
20/02/16 Cash sales £4,200.
24/02/16 Paid £2,900 of the cash into the bank.
28/02/16 Paid wages £1,000 (cash).
29/02/16 Paid rent £1,000 (cheque).
Note: The balance on the discounts allowed account as at 1 February was £810, and the balance on the discounts received account as at 1 February was £900.
Required:
a) Write up the three column cash book to record the above transactions.
b) Update the discounts allowed and discounts received accounts.

QUESTION SIX
Write short notes on FOUR of the following:
   a) Share capital
   b) VAT
   c) Working capital
   d) A petty cash system
   e) The role of a bookkeeper
   f) Public finance

QUESTION SEVEN
The following are the first 12 transactions of a new business:
Feb. 01 Put £48,000 into a business bank account.
Feb. 01 Paid rent £1,400 by cheque.
Feb. 01 Paid £22,000 for equipment, paying by cheque.
Feb. 02 Bought goods for resale £7,500, paying by cheque.
Feb. 03 Bought stationery for £600, paying by cheque.
Feb. 06 Sold goods for £4,600, and immediately banked the cheque.
Feb. 08 Paid wages £900, paying by cheque.
Feb. 13 Bought goods for resale £5,500, paying by cheque.
Feb. 15 Paid insurance premiums £1,750, paying by cheque.
Feb. 16 Sold goods for £6,000, and immediately banked the cheque.
Feb. 17 Paid wages £850, paying by cheque.
Feb. 21 Sold goods for £3,000 and immediately banked the cheque.
Required:
a) Record the above transactions in the relevant ledger account, and balance the accounts off.
b) Prepare the trial balance as at the end of February 2016.
c) Explain the principal functions of a trial balance.

By the time you finish reading this book, you should be able to:

I.   Record journal entries accurately.

II.   Prepare financial statements i.e income statement, balance sheet.

III.   Prepare main types of cash book i.e two column cash book and three column cash book.

IV.   Prepare cash flow statements.

V.   Prepare company accounts, manufacturing accounts and partnership accounts.

VI.   Know the various methods of calculating depreciation.

VII.   Know various types of ratios and how to calculate them.

VIII.   Prepare property, plant and equipment schedule.

IX.   Prepare control accounts and Bank Reconciliation Statement.

Made in United States
North Haven, CT
30 April 2023